Did You Hear?

Karen J. Guralnick
Illustrated by Reggie Holladay

Rigby®

A Harcourt Achieve Imprint

www.Rigby.com
1-800-531-5015

One morning as Berta and her twin brother Sergio were on their way to school, Berta stopped suddenly. Sergio asked her what was wrong, but Berta couldn't speak.

"Berta, stop joking around," said Sergio, "or we'll be late for school."

Berta knew that she had to warn Sergio of the huge snake that was coming near them, but she couldn't say anything because she was too afraid that the snake would get them.

"What is wrong with you?" asked Sergio.

When Berta was finally able to speak, she shouted, "SNAKE!"

"What are you talking about?" asked Sergio.

"Don't you see it over by the huge rock?" asked Berta as she tried to hide behind her brother.

"I don't think it will bite," said Sergio with a big grin on his face.

"How do you know?" asked Berta closing her eyes.

4

"Look at it closely," said Sergio.

Berta opened her eyes just in time to see Mr. Kania pulling a garden hose through the grass.

"Well, Berta, not only is Mr. Kania a school custodian, but he's a snake handler, too," Sergio teased.

"Very funny," said Berta, as her face became very red.

By recess, Berta had forgotten all about the "snake." She and her friends were sitting on the swings, and they began talking about the plans that they had for Friday night.

"I can't wait to go to the music store," said Mai.

"I am so happy that you found out that Rick Eebee has a new CD coming out, Berta," said Sarah.

"I wish that I could get him to sign the poster that I have of him," said Berta.

"I just want to ask him where he gets his ideas for the songs that he writes and sings," said Mai.

While Berta and her friends were talking, Sergio was telling his friends about what had happened with Berta that morning.

"I can hardly believe that Berta thought that she had seen a snake," said Jamil.

"I've never seen anyone as scared as she was," said Sergio.

"You should have let her think that the snake was going to bite her when she closed her eyes," added Jason.

"Yeah, that would have been really funny," said Jamil.

Peng, who was a girl from the twins' class, was playing soccer near Sergio and his friends. She heard some of what they said and rushed over to tell her friends.

"Guess what?" asked Peng. "I heard Sergio talking about Berta seeing a snake that almost bit her."

The three girls gasped and looked over at Berta.

"Wow," said Ellie, "I wonder how she got away."

The three girls continued whispering about Berta. Every few minutes they would stop talking, look over at Berta, and point. Berta wondered why Peng and her friends kept looking and pointing at her.

Then the bell rang, and the children had to go inside. Once inside, Berta's teacher said that it was time for writing. Berta was so excited to continue writing her letter to Rick Eebee that she forgot all about Peng and her friends. After a while, Berta started to get a headache, so she put her head on her desk for the rest of writing time.

When it was almost time to go home, Berta's teacher told them that they wouldn't have any homework that night. Everyone in the class cheered except Berta.

"Aren't you glad that there's no homework tonight?" asked Mai.

"I am glad. It's just that my head hurts," said Berta.

"Maybe you should go home and take a nap instead of coming over to my house today," said Mai.

"I think I'll do that," said Berta. "I'm sorry that I won't be able to help you bake cookies."

"That's OK," said Mai.

The students were lined up by the door to go to their lockers. All Berta could think about was going home and getting into bed. She was glad that she didn't have to talk to anyone on her way home.

When Berta got home, she explained that she had a headache and wanted to take a nap instead of going to Mai's house. Her mom said that it was a good idea and that she would come and check on her soon. Berta went upstairs, got into bed, and fell asleep.

Two hours later, Berta was still sleeping. Her mom was worried about her, so she woke Berta up. Berta could barely lift up her head, and she was shivering under the blanket.

"Let's see if you have a fever," said Berta's mom. "Wow, your fever is 102 degrees. I'll call the doctor and see if I can give you some medicine."

Berta nodded. She didn't even mind that she might not be able to get Rick Eebee's CD on Friday. At the same time that Berta's mom came upstairs with the medicine, Sergio came home from basketball practice.

"Mom," Sergio called, "I don't feel very well."

"Your sister is sick, and you probably have the same thing. Come upstairs to your room, and I'll be there in a minute," replied Mom.

Sergio's fever was also 102 degrees, so Mom went downstairs, got some more medicine, and brought it to him. Standing between the two rooms, Mom said, "Well, I guess that both of you will be staying home from school tomorrow."

The next morning, Berta and Sergio were feeling a little better. As Berta was taking out a book to read, Sergio walked into the room.

"Too bad you can't go to school today. Maybe you would have seen another *scary* animal," Sergio said laughing.

"Ha, ha, ha," said Berta with a mad look on her face. She had almost forgotten about the "snake" from the day before.

"You didn't tell anyone did you?" asked Berta.

"I only told a couple of my friends," replied Sergio.

Berta sighed, opened her book, and
began reading. Sergio realized that
Berta was not happy, so he went back
to his room.

That day at school, three boys were talking about Berta.

"Have you seen her today?" asked Marc.

"No, have you seen her?" asked Mario.

"After she was bitten by the snake, she probably had to go to the hospital," said Todd.

"And I haven't seen Sergio, either. Maybe he's with her at the hospital," said Marc.

Berta was also being talked about across the hall.

"I heard that she got attacked by a dog with really big teeth," said Yen.

"Was she badly hurt?" asked Laura.

"I don't know. Maybe we should ask her brother."

"I haven't seen him this morning. Maybe he had to stay home to help take care of her."

The next day, Berta and Sergio were still sick, so they had to stay home again. At school even the teachers began talking about Berta.

"Did you hear about Berta?" asked Mr. Loomis.

"She was very brave," said Mrs. Ching.

"We should have our second grade classes make cards for her," said Mr. Loomis.

"That's a great idea," said Mrs. Ching. "I'll take them to her house after school today."

Later that afternoon, the doorbell rang at Berta's house. Berta's mom answered the door and invited Mrs. Ching inside.

"Some of our students heard about Berta and made get-well cards for her."

Berta's mom looked confused because nobody had ever made the children cards when they were sick before.

Berta's mom said, "Thank you," and Mrs. Ching left.

Mom went upstairs to Berta's room and told her that Mrs. Ching had come and brought her some cards created by the second graders. Berta opened up the first card and read it aloud:

Dear Berta,
I heard that you were attacked by a bear. I hope you feel better soon.
From,
Andrew

Get Well

"Why does that boy think that you were attacked by a bear?" asked Mom, laughing.

"I don't know," said Berta, shrugging her shoulders.

"Why don't you look at more cards?" suggested Mom. "Maybe that boy just has a big imagination."

Each card said something about Berta being attacked by a different animal.

"Are you sure that you have no idea why all of these kids think that you were attacked?" asked Mom.

"Yes, I'm sure, but maybe Sergio knows something," said Berta.

Mom called Sergio into the room and asked him if he knew why these kids would think that his sister had been attacked by an animal. Sergio thought for a minute and then began to smile. "I think I know what happened," he said, and he began to tell his mom about what had happened with the hose.

"I think that someone heard me telling the story and then told someone else," said Sergio. "I guess that the story was changed as each person retold it. Since Berta hasn't been in school for two days, they probably think that she is recovering from a terrible animal bite!"

"Well, Sergio," said Mom, laughing, "since *you* told the story, *you* should be the one to explain what really happened."

"Yeah," said Berta, "and this time make sure that everybody hears the *same* story."